EDMUND THOMAS CHIPP

'A life that led melodious days'

José Hopkins

This paperback edition first published 2013

Published jointly by José Hopkins
and Cambridge Editions
Unit 2, Burr Elm Court
Main Street, Caldecote
Cambridge CB23 7NU

ISBN 978-0-9576358-0-7

Produced by Cambridge Publishing Management Limited.

Printed and bound in Dorchester by Henry Ling Limited.

Contents

Illustrations

Foreword

I am very pleased to commend José Hopkins's celebration of the life and career of Dr. Edmund Chipp, Organist of Ely Cathedral from 1866 to 1886. This monograph is long overdue.

It is fitting that José should be writing this as Organ Adviser for the Diocese of Ely. One of Chipp's published pieces was in honour of St. Etheldreda, our Patron Saint and Foundress of the original community in Ely.

My cursory study of Dr. Chipp's life reveals a man committed to the spiritual traditions of organ playing and choral music at the service of the Church of England. Moreover, he was a talented and dedicated musician in the widest possible sphere to whom we owe access to many of Mendelssohn's scores, as well as specifically bringing Mendelssohn's organ work to public performance for the first time in the United Kingdom.

There is a modest memorial to Dr. Chipp close to the organ loft in the Cathedral. I believe that Mrs. Hopkins's book will prove an even wider and more accessible memorial to him.

+Stephen Ely

Preface

My introduction to Edmund Thomas Chipp must have been through an organ, namely the one which he played at Holy Trinity, Paddington, between 1856 and 1862 and which, after its lengthy stay in Ely, I have subsequently been able to enjoy in my local parish church in Haslingfield.

In researching the life of this nineteenth-century organist and composer I have been greatly helped by Mrs. Elizabeth Stazicker, Archivist of Ely Cathedral; Peter Meadows and the staff of the Manuscripts Department, Cambridge University Library; Dr. John Kitchen in Edinburgh; Dr. Nicholas Thistlethwaite and Mr. David Byers in Belfast; but above all I would like to thank Anne Page for continual encouragement, and my husband Harold for much patience and practical help. In the final stages invaluable editorial assistance from Karen Beaulah and Lucy Metzger is gratefully acknowledged.

José Hopkins
Haslingfield
September 2013

1
E.T. Chipp (1823-1886)
'A life that led melodious days'

The quotation, originally from Tennyson's *In Memoriam*, is taken from Edmund Thomas Chipp's memorial tablet near the stairs to the organ loft in Ely Cathedral, the only memorial to a musician in the Cathedral. His melodious days would have begun very early in his life since his father, Thomas Paul Chipp (1793-1870), had sung in Westminster Abbey Choir in London, and had learned the piano under Clementi. He became a harpist and drummer and was a member of all the principal London orchestras, having the distinction of playing at the Coronations of George IV, William IV and Victoria. The family lived in Albany Street, St. Pancras, in 1841.[1] Edmund was the eldest of five children. His brother Horatio was also a professional musician, playing the cello.

Edmund Chipp is remembered now for his years at Ely Cathedral as Organist (1866-1886) and for his organ music. His musical career began, however, as a chorister at the Chapel Royal under William Hawes between the ages of seven and seventeen, during which time he sang at Queen Victoria's Coronation. Chipp studied the organ under George Cooper, Sr. (Organist of St. Paul's Cathedral), and the violin under J.B. Nadaud and Tolbecque. As a violinist he played in various orchestras, including Her Majesty's Private Band, and he also held a succession of organ appointments in London (the Albany Chapel, Regent's Park; the Italian Opera House,

Haymarket; the Percy Chapel, Tottenham Court Road; and St. John's Chapel, Downshire Hill, Hampstead) before succeeding Dr. Gauntlett as Organist of St. Olave's, Southwark, in 1847. He moved to St. Mary-at-Hill in the City of London in 1852 and then to Holy Trinity, Paddington, in 1856, and succeeded W.T. Best as Organist at the Royal Panopticon of Science and Art, Leicester Square, in 1855. During this time he took a music degree at Cambridge (St. John's College) in 1859 and obtained a Mus.D. in June 1860, the first doctorate in music under Sir William Sterndale Bennett and the first in eight years. Since personal examinations for Cambridge music degrees were only introduced in 1857, Chipp was one of the earliest to be so examined.

Leaving London in 1862, Chipp crossed the Irish Sea to Belfast where he stayed until 1866 as Organist of St. George's Church and the Ulster Hall, as well as conducting the Anacreontic Society, the Classical Harmonists and the Vocal Union. He then moved to Scotland, where he was briefly Organist of the Kinnaird Hall, Dundee, and St. Paul's Church, Edinburgh, before being appointed to Ely Cathedral in 1867.[2]

Chipp married Emily Jane Oliver (1824–1899), the daughter of a hotel keeper on Hampstead Heath, on 30 August 1848 at St. John's Church, Hampstead.[3] At the time of the 1851 Census the couple were living with his mother-in-law, Mary Oliver, at Chestnut Cottage in the Vale of Health in Hampstead, north London, now a Grade II listed building. From the evidence of works written there, this would appear to have been his home until his move to Belfast, although some works were written at 3 Norfolk Villas, Bayswater. There were four children of the marriage. The eldest son, Herbert, was an artist and a noted lawn tennis player, Emily never married, Mary died in infancy, and the youngest, Charles Percy Oliver, became a wine merchant, following in his mother's family tradition.

Shortly before the end of his life Chipp received a Fellowship (*honoris causa*) from the College of Organists. His last public

Chestnut Cottage, Vale of Health, Hampstead Heath, 2007

performances in London were at the Bow and Bromley recitals and at the Henry Smart Memorial recital at the Royal College of Music, although no details have been traced.

Edmund Chipp died at Nice on 17 December 1886. During the first week of December he had left England for the south of France, having been 'seeking restoration in rest and change since the middle of September. His remains were brought back to England and he was buried in the family grave at Highgate Cemetery on Christmas Eve, 1886.'[4] Notices of his passing appeared in the *London Daily News* (24 December), the *Bath Chronicle* (30 December), the *Liverpool Mercury* (30 December) and the *Belfast News-Letter* (20 December).

2
THE MUSIC

The archive of Chipp's music manuscripts at Cambridge University Library[5] contains oratorios, anthems, cantatas and service music, choral music with organ, organ arrangements, works for organ solo, piano solos and arrangements, and songs, in all 213 items. There are also volumes of manuscript and published music by Chipp in Ely Cathedral Music Library, consisting mainly of service music. Analysis of the organ and piano arrangements shows overwhelmingly that Mendelssohn was the greatest inspiration for these (ten), followed by Bach and Handel (four each), Mozart (three), Spohr, Weber and Beethoven (two each), and Schumann, Schubert, Gounod, Wagner, Heller, Molique and Horsley each providing the source for one arrangement. One of the Spohr arrangements, 'Destroyed in Babylon' from *The Last Judgement*, was included in *Organist's Manual* (1851-52), edited by George Cooper Jr., son of Chipp's tutor.[6] An indication of Chipp's popularity after his death may be gained from the fact that his works received 322 performances during the period 1880 to 1930. In June 1900 the Birmingham Town Hall organist gave a recital of music selected by the audience, for which the 1899 voting was firstly Wagner's *Tannhäuser* overture, secondly Lemmens' *Storm Fantasia* and thirdly Chipp's *Variations on an Austrian Hymn (God Preserve the Emperor)*.[7]

Further reference to Chipp's keyboard works will be made in Chapter 4, but his choral music and his three oratorios in particular deserve consideration. *Job,* completed on 31 December 1859 at Chestnut Cottage, Hampstead, was his Cambridge Mus.D. submission and was performed in Cambridge on 21 June 1860.[8] John Sims Reeves, leading tenor, had volunteered to sing the tenor part, but was unable to do so; in the event Wilbye Cooper deputised. A pamphlet of the text was produced, together with a full score and piano score. A conducting score was produced in 1864, and the presence of pencil marks of names of performers may indicate that a later performance took place. There is a *col organo* indication at one point. His wife, Emily Jane Chipp, selected the words from Isaiah and from the Psalms. The first chorus of 'Evil Angels' ('Call thou if there be any that answer thee') hints at the Baal Chorus in Mendelssohn's *Elijah*. In fact, a report abridged from *The Northern Whig* of 9 December 1865 indicates that a performance of *Job*, described as a first performance, took place in Belfast on 8 December 1865.[9] Chipp of course conducted, and Dr. Stewart, the organist of St. Patrick's Cathedral, Dublin, accompanied the Belfast Vocal Union on the Ulster Hall organ. The review affirmed, 'as a conductor Dr. Chipp is almost unequalled … the execution of the work was highly satisfactory.'

Naomi, written at Ely in 1868 and dedicated to Sir Michael Costa, was also published, and a conducting score exists in Cambridge. *Israel in Babylon*, composed at various times in 1871, although with one section marked 1862, was also published. Manuscript scores survive in Cambridge, one full score orchestrated by Arthur Carwall and one with piano accompaniment.

The manuscript songs held in Cambridge number thirty-four individual items plus two collections of three and four songs respectively. Collaboration with his wife is evident in the song 'Violets' written in Belfast and Ely, for which she provided the words, and in a four-part *Ode to Shakespeare, In Memoriam April 23rd, 1564* written in Belfast, with poetry by Emily. Chipp's son Herbert provided the words for 'The Seaman's Song,' written in 1874. There is a tremendous variety of subject matter in the song collection, from 'The Charge of the Light Brigade' (1860) to settings of words by Schiller, Scott and Shelley.

Service music includes numerous settings of canticles and Psalms, anthems, and a Processional Hymn written for the Ely Diocesan Church Music Society in 1874, although without words, plus two anthems for the St. Etheldreda Celebration in Ely in 1873, referred to below. He also compiled a collection of chants, canticle settings and hymns by himself and various other composers, *Music for the Church Service and Home Circle*, in 1866. This was judged to be a useful collection for parish churches, intended as it was for churches where simple chants were no longer sufficient fare for choirs who desired something more challenging, but not necessarily of cathedral standard. Many examples of the use of his service music appeared in notices of services in cathedrals and parish churches for several years after his death.

3
Chipp and Mendelssohn

Dr. Chipp was an early champion of Mendelssohn's music and of his organ sonatas in particular, which were slow to catch on in England. The sonatas were published in 1845, and Chipp was probably the first English organist to play them in public, at a concert in Walker's organ factory in April 1846. He even performed all six from memory on 13 December 1848 at Hill's organ works, in a concert which also included other items.[10] The *Musical Times*, writing about the sonatas after Chipp's death, noted that he:

> *played the whole of Mendelssohn's Six Organ Sonatas entirely from memory. The programme on that occasion was Bach's Toccata and Fugue in F and C sharp minor fugue from the 48; two works by Hesse (including God Save the Queen), Chipp's Introduction and Air Varied; and as arrangements Handel's 'He rebuked the red sea,' Beethoven's 'Adelaide' and a slow movement from one of Mendelssohn's symphonies.*

Mendelssohn himself, according to the account, considered playing all six sonatas in one go too fatiguing. Chipp also played the third sonata to Mendelssohn on the organ at the Hanover Square Rooms, and the *Musical Times* noted Mendelssohn's comment:

> *I have heard Mr. E. Chipp perform on the organ and the manner in which he played one of the most difficult of my*

> *Organ Sonatas has given me a very high opinion of his talents and his skill as a musician and as a performer.*[11]

Chipp performed one of the sonatas at a Birmingham Musical Festival concert in 1849; a review commented:

> *Mr. Chipp played it like a great disciple of the great musician and greatest of organ players, and the impression he produced was a flattering tribute to his ability and taste.*[12]

Chipp's obituary expressly stated that 'between 1850 and 1855 he constructed with his own hand, from the single parts, full scores of all Mendelssohn's works which were not then published in that form.' This was apparently achieved during the 'leisure' time at his disposal whilst a member of Her Majesty's Private Band.

Chipp dedicated no. 13 of his *24 Sketches* to Mendelssohn ('In Memoriam F.M.B.'), and arranged movements from Mendelssohn's Third and Fourth Symphonies, which were published. His own music inevitably flourished in the post-Mendelssohn tradition, and his concert programmes constantly reflected his mentor.

His piano pieces too reflect Mendelssohn's influence; in particular the *Twilight Fancies*, Op. 12, show an affinity to that composer's *Songs Without Words*, as illustrated in a comment by Temperley:

> *Songs without Words school: outstanding set in this category; not entirely original, often borrowing from Mendelssohn, Schumann and Bennett. Sometimes too honeyed in sentiment, but have a delicate poetry worthy of their models, a sensitivity to the finer subtleties of piano music that place them as high art.*[13]

A more exhaustive analysis of these pieces appeared in *The Musical World*.[14] Two of the pieces have been recorded (London Piano School vol. 3, Arabesque Recordings).

4
Music for Organ and Piano

The *24 Sketches*, Op. 11, conceived as a collection of short pieces in free style for church or chamber organ, are accessible and useful pieces for present-day organists and arguably Chipp's most popular organ music. Published in 1855 and costing 15/-, they bear markings presumably relevant to the organ at St. Mary-at-Hill, where Chipp was Organist at the time. The Subscribers' Edition of all twenty-four pieces was dedicated to Sir Frederick Gore Ouseley, and was so popular that it was later reissued in two parts by Dalmaine. Subscribers included leading organ builders - Gray & Davison, Hill, Holdich, Nicholson, and Jardine & Kirtland. An edition was made by J.E. West for the *Original Compositions for the Organ* series (1907) of five of the *24 Sketches* (nos. 10, 12, 16, 23, 24). Purcell J. Mansfield produced an edition of numbers 1-12 in 1936, in which he took responsibility for all markings, and provided registration suggestions for a three-manual organ and pedals, whereas Chipp usually specified for two manuals. Mansfield also took the trouble to produce alternative ways of managing the abnormal stretches referred to below. A full list of the twenty-four pieces is in Annex 1.

A Subscribers' Edition of *Compositions for the Organ* edited by Garrett and Higgs was published in 1888, in which the editors stated that they had:

made a selection from a very large number of MS compositions for the organ left by their eminent and lamented friend, Dr. E.T. Chipp. They believe that the intrinsic merit of these works and the mastery they show over so many forms of composition will make them welcome, not only to those who can remember the brilliant performances of their composer, but to all who can appreciate true organ music, solid in style and legitimate in effect.

Editorial suggestions were printed at the bottom of the page in order to preserve the integrity of the original pieces. No organ builders were listed as subscribers this time, but rather such leading names from the world of music as Stainer, Sullivan and Stanford. A collection of sixteen pieces of organ music in manuscript form exists in Cambridge, some marked 'published' and some numbered in blue crayon. Thirteen of these were published in the Garrett and Higgs 1888 edition. In 1936 a Mansfield edition of Chipp's organ music, *Compositions for the Organ*, Book 2, *Miscellaneous Solos*, was published. The pieces included in this volume were intended not just for service use but also to be suitable for recitals. Three of the *24 Sketches* (nos. 16, 21 and 24) were included here.

At first glance it will be seen that some of the titles of the twenty-four are reminiscent of Mendelssohn pieces, e.g. 'Andante religioso', (no. 1). No. 13, 'In memoriam F.M.B.', indeed refers to his mentor. There are two pieces entitled 'In memoriam M.F.G.C.', one in B minor (no. 2) marked *dolente*, which also exists in manuscript in a piano version, and the other in F minor marked *molto adagio e lento*. M.F.G.C. was his daughter, Mary Florence Grace, who died on 12 May 1852 aged one year.

Chipp's penchant for using remote keys is revealed in no. 7, 'Andante' in E♭ minor, and other instances occur elsewhere. This particular piece also contains an example of an extended interval, in this case a minor tenth, and the use of such intervals probably indicates that Chipp possessed an abnormal stretch. The

'Pastorale' in A major, no. 12, is reminiscent of Mendelssohn (Andante from Sonata No. 3) and is the longest piece among the twelve published by Mansfield in 1936.

In some of these short pieces the composer has begun to evolve an organ style often with an independent pedal line rather than simply echoing his piano writing. No. 2 ('In memoriam M.F.G.C.') has a pedal line which is the bass line of the piano version penned at Windsor in 1852, this time in G♭ minor. A letter from Chipp written in 1879 reveals that he intended 'some day' to produce another book 'but of a different character altogether.'[15] The intention seems not to have been realised in his lifetime, but it may be that the 1888 collection edited by Garrett and Higgs fulfilled this intention, since it was published only two years after his death. A review of the *24 Sketches* concluded, 'If Sketch No. 1 is played through we can guarantee that none of its 23 companions will be passed over.'[16]

The organ work that did much to establish Chipp's reputation as a performer was the set of variations, Op. 2, on Haydn's Austrian hymn, *God Preserve the Emperor*. The piece, written while Chipp was Organist at St. Olave's, Southwark, was composed for and first performed at the Grand Musical Festival held at Birmingham in 1849, and was dedicated to Michael Costa and published by Dalmaine. The original copy included the specification of the organ. The actual concert was the Second Miscellaneous Concert on Wednesday 5 September and opened with Chipp playing his Variations, followed by a song by Spohr, and possibly other organ pieces. There are seven variations, starting with a fast and furious Introduction in G minor, leading into the theme in G major. Variation 6 reverts to G minor, with a gentler feel. All are in common time, with the exception of Variations 5 and 7 in triple time. Virtuoso pedal passages occur, as well as semiquaver passages in both hands. The final Variation, marked *allegro maestoso e con fuoco*, has continuous quaver chromatic movement in the pedals, some, in octaves. The piece featured frequently in his subsequent recitals, and was republished by Novello in 1870, price 2s. 6d.[17] A provisional list of Chipp's published organ music is appended at Annex 2.

Piano solos in manuscript form number sixty-six in one collection, with a further twenty-nine solos and duets filed separately. In the first collection is 'In memoriam M.F.G.C.', referred to above, with a pencil annotation 'published in 24 Sketches in B minor.' 'Inquietude Impromptu', written in Bayswater in 1857, has the intriguing annotation 'Reminiscence of a committee meeting.' 'Marriage Bells', (Belfast, 1864) is virtually identical to 'St. Mary's Bells', (Ely, 1880), found in the second collection, and 'Marriage Bells', (Ely, 1878, a duet). Chipp would certainly have heard the bells of St. Mary's Church, Ely, from his house on Palace Green. A Miss Higgs, possibly acting as a publisher, must have examined the collection at some point since there are pencil annotations to this effect. Holiday locations (Thun, Switzerland and Bournemouth) are also revealed. 'The mysterious quadrilles', September 1845, perhaps indicates Chipp's involvement in the 'dance band' world as a source of income at that time, although this form of employment was a relatively lowly one in the ranks of professional musicians.

5
Chipp as a Performer

Chipp's skill as a performer is evident from the words of Basil Harwood, who succeeded him as Organist of Ely Cathedral:

> *To my great regret I never had a chance of hearing him play. He was well known as a very fine organist with remarkable skill in pedalling. Soon after my appointment I received a letter of congratulation from Mr. Gambier Parry, the father of Sir Hubert Parry, and himself a good judge of music, in which he speaks of the delight with which, while engaged in painting the roof, he had often listened to Dr. Chipp's 'glorious music' rolling down the nave.*[18]

William Glover, too, in his *Memoirs of a Cambridge Chorister*, also considered it worth noting that he had heard Chipp play at St. Olave's during his tenure there.[19]

Mention has already been made of Chipp's performances of the Mendelssohn organ sonatas. Various references to his recitals have been traced; one at the Birmingham Musical Festival in 1849 has already been mentioned. Another one was his programme for the first of the popular concerts on the Mulholland Grand Organ in the Ulster Hall, Belfast, on Saturday 20 December 1862, when his programme was as follows:

Balfe: *Overture to Lover's Well*
Chipp: *Chanson* (Study No. 2)
Bach: *Fugue St. Ann's* [sic]
Handel: *Hallelujah Chorus* (Messiah)
Chipp: *Fantasia* (The Harmonious Blacksmith)
Pleyel: *Andante*
Mendelssohn: *Sonata No. 1*
National Anthem *God Save the Queen* (varied)[20]

Another programme that survives was in a review of his concert, part of a daily series in the specially built Exhibition Hall, Old Trafford, Manchester, in 1857 for the Exhibition of Art Treasures of the United Kingdom, which has never been surpassed as the largest art exhibition in the world. There is a similarity with the Belfast programme quoted above in that it includes transcriptions, works

Kirtland & Jardine organ at the Exhibition of Art Treasures of the United Kingdom, Manchester, 1857 (courtesy of Manchester Libraries Information and Archives, Manchester City Council)

by Mendelssohn, and his own compositions, and indeed this mixture continues throughout his recital career:

Handel: *Overture, Adagio, March*
'Occasional Oratorio'
Pleyel: Movement from a Quartet
Mendelssohn: *Adagio, Third Symphony*
Balfe: *Overture 'Geraldine'*
Chipp: *Study in G*
Costa: *March 'Eli'*
Bach: *Fugue in D*
Mendelssohn: *Andante con moto from*
Fourth Symphony
Chipp: *Fantasia 'God Save the Emperor'*
National Anthem

The organ specifically built for the duration of the exhibition (May to October) was by Kirtland & Jardine, and the specification is shown in Annex 3. The only expense traceable from the Report of the Exhibition Executive Committee is £337 for the organ screen, the organ having been erected solely at the builder's expense.[21] Winterhalter's portraits of Queen Victoria and Prince Albert were hung on either side of the organ. Chipp's recital took place on Tuesday 13 October, the day that recorded the highest attendance of the whole exhibition (29,160). The review of the concert asserts that he ranks 'in the first class and in some particulars outstrips his competitors ... Never since the erection of that noble instrument by Messrs. Kirtland & Jardine have its capabilities been more elaborately displayed. For two hours Mr. Chipp attracted to the vicinity of the organ thousands of admirers of sweet sounds.'[22]

He participated along with other performers in the opening of the new organ by John Nicholson in the Concert Room, Worcester, on 29 November 1854,[23] and he re-opened the organ at Bakewell in November 1859.[24] Another new organ which he opened was at

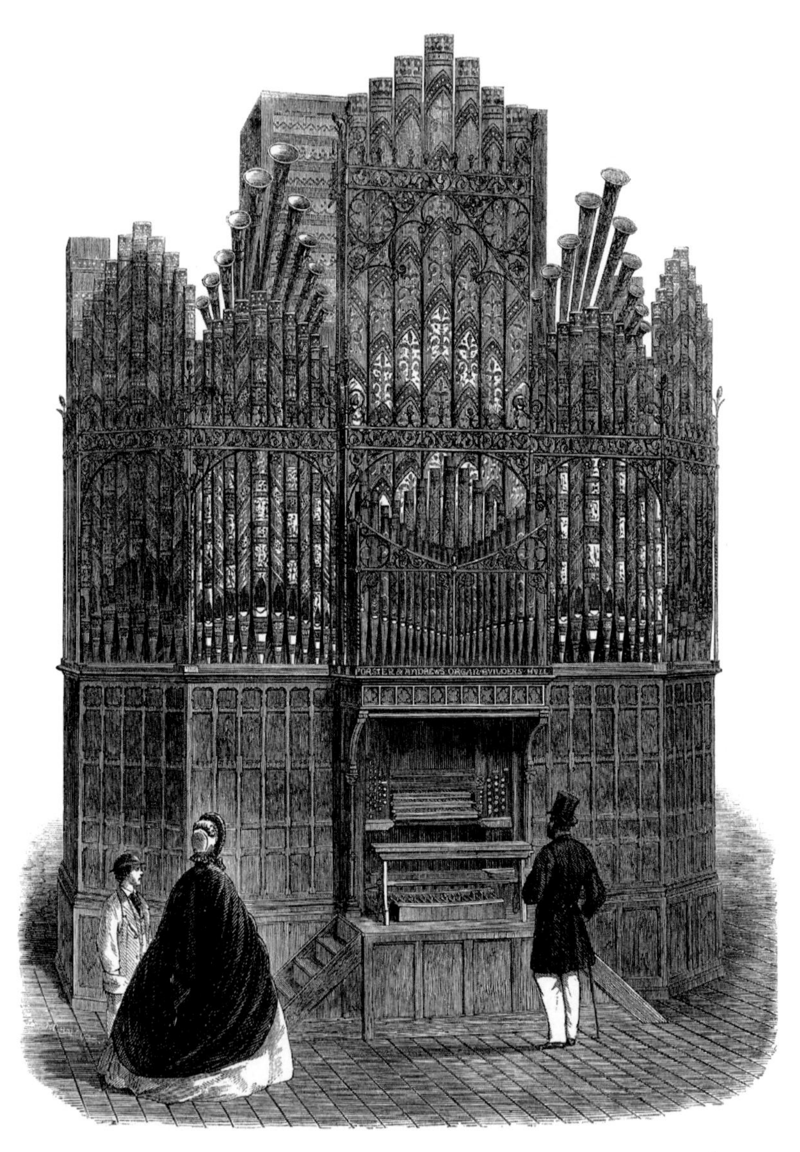

Church organ, made by Forster & Andrews of Hull, England, exhibited at the 1862 International Exhibition in London; contemporary wood engraving (The Granger Collection, New York)

St. Mary's Church, Leicester, on 16 October 1860, when he was described as 'of St. John's College, Cambridge.'[25] Chipp wrote an enthusiastic testimonial the following year for Forster & Andrews, who were responsible for the organ, having never previously encountered their work,[26] and he later wrote another undated one having become more acquainted with it. This could well have been written after his concerts at the International Exhibition in 1862 (see below).[27] The Crystal Palace was another huge venue where Chipp played for a service, at which the Rev. C.H. Spurgeon, the noted Baptist preacher, preached for thirty-eight minutes. Chipp accompanied a congregation of over 23,000 people.[28]

Chipp performed at the International Exhibition of 1862 in South Kensington on the organ erected by Forster & Andrews; he:

> *attracted crowds by his masterly playing and delighted musicians by his selections, which invariably included pieces suited to the instrument, and never condescended to the trivial exhibitions of which we have had many examples in the same building.*

Chipp was a regular recitalist on Wednesday and Saturday afternoons, and had given the first recital on the instrument at 3 pm on 31 May 1862. His association with the instrument helped to attract much praise for it at the time.[29]

Bach fugues, Handel, Mendelssohn and oratorio choruses appeared in Chipp's recitals, in contrast to the more trivial operatic selections of other performers. He gave another concert that year at Waltham Abbey on 3 November, when he played Mendelssohn and arrangements of Costa, Bach, Haydn and Handel.[30]

Chipp's skill as a violinist should not be forgotten, and a violin made by Andreas Fisher with an inscription inside 'in homage dedicated to Edmund Thomas Chipp, church choirmaster in Edinburgh' survives to this day in private hands in Belgium. He was for a time

(1843–55) a member of Her Majesty's Private Band, and some of his compositions or arrangements were completed while he was at Windsor, in addition to arrangements of Mendelssohn. One such is the transcription of Gounod's *Marche Nuptiale* for organ and three trombones, for the marriage of HRH the Duke of Albany, fourth son of Queen Victoria, in April 1882, perhaps implying that Chipp himself played the organ on that occasion, although he had left Court service by that time.

Chipp's association with Her Majesty's Private Band, an appointment which had been sought for him by his father, was the subject of much public attention in the *Musical World* in 1855, when the circumstances of his leaving the Band were made public.[31] Both he and his brother Horatio the cellist were members of the Royal Orchestra, but the latter resigned and Edmund was dismissed. The

The organ at the Royal Panopticon, London, *The Builder*, 1854 (courtesy of Cambridge University Library)

source of the disquiet was remuneration for service as a member of the Band and an unsatisfactory relationship with the conductor of the Band, G.F.Anderson, who disbursed such remuneration. In addition to the loss of income of between £80 and £100 paid to be in readiness for Her Majesty's commands, the £45 per annum warrant money also disappeared when members left the Band. For these sums they were expected to reside at Windsor for the greater part of the winter, with no compensation for the upkeep of their accommodation in town. As part of the account which Chipp himself gave at that time, he had also acted in 1847 as Deputy Organist to Her Majesty's Private Chapel, and:

> *After I had continued in that capacity for some time, Mr. Anderson enquired what salary I received as Organist at Mr. Montgomery's Chapel. I replied £40 per annum. Mr.Anderson enquired whether I should be satisfied with the same sum at Her Majesty's Private Chapel to which I acceded.*

However, Anderson's nephew Cusins was appointed. Then, at Anderson's request Chipp prepared the design that was adopted for the new organ at the Private Chapel, but for which Anderson took the credit, without even asking Chipp to inspect it. The *Musical World* through this protracted series of revelations supported Chipp in glowing terms:

> *His eminent talent as a musician is unanimously acknowledged in the profession and his conduct as a gentleman in public and private life we have every reason to believe beyond reproach.*

Later in 1855 the *Musical World* published a review of 'Three Romances' by Chipp, dedicated to Mrs.Anderson, perhaps a sign of a rapprochement?[32]

Chipp became organist of the Hill organ in the Royal Panopticon of Science and Art in Leicester Square in 1855, with daily recitals, succeeding W.T. Best. Best had used the title 'Organist and Professor

Extract from arrangement for organ by E.T. Chipp of Mendelssohn 'Choral and Fuga', Op. 96 (courtesy of Cambridge University Library)

of the Organ at the Royal Panopticon,' but it is not clear whether Chipp inherited that designation. On 27 January 1856 a commemoration of the centenary of Mozart's birth took place at the Panopticon. In the morning Chipp played transcriptions consisting of an aria from *The Marriage of Figaro*, the Andante from Quartet No. 6, a sonata, a chorus from a litany, and an aria from *Idomeneo.* In the evening a second concert took place with items from soloists, and the Orpheus Glee Union, accompanied by Chipp on the organ.[33] The following month saw a tribute to Handel with a performance of *Acis and Galatea,* again with the Orpheus Glee Union and with accompaniment provided by Chipp on the organ. The notice remarked that Chipp's performances 'may be reckoned amongst the staple attractions of the Royal Panopticon.'[34] The

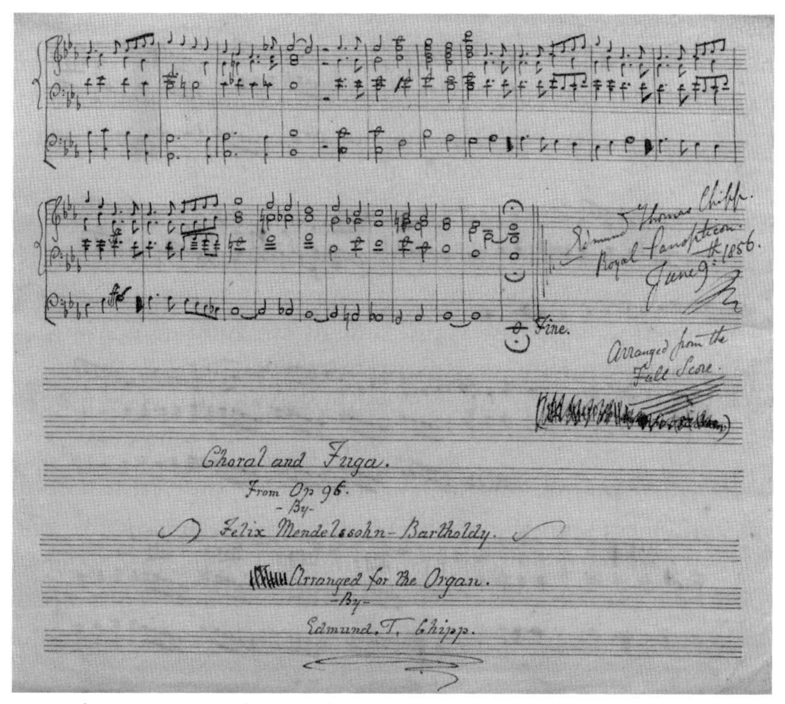

Extract from arrangement for organ by E.T. Chipp of Mendelssohn 'Choral and Fuga', Op. 96 (continued)

Panopticon closed, however, in 1856, having been open for only two years, and having attracted thousands of visitors per day. The organ, which it was claimed was the largest in the world at that time, ultimately went to St. Paul's Cathedral. An arrangement finished whilst Chipp was working there, as noted on the manuscript, was the Choral and Fugue from Mendelssohn's Op. 96 (Hymn for alto, chorus and orchestra), arranged 'from the full score.'

6

BELFAST AND THE MULHOLLAND GRAND ORGAN

The installation of the Mulholland Grand Organ in the newly established Ulster Hall, Belfast, had been a matter of public interest in Belfast well before its inauguration during the Belfast Musical Festival in December 1862. The organ was a gift to the Ulster Hall Company from Andrew Mulholland, a former Lord Mayor. One of the objectives of his philanthropy had been:

> *To give an opportunity to the working classes to hear from time to time the best music from a truly splendid instrument at such a rate as would enable the humblest artisan to enjoy advantages which even the opulent could but rarely purchase until now.*[35]

Built by William Hill & Son, London, the organ had at its opening four manuals and pedal with 62 stops, and had been secured by a donation of £3,500. The three sets of bellows were each operated by two men.

Edmund Chipp had been appointed as Organist of the Ulster Hall and Conductor of the associated musical groups, as well as to St. George's Church earlier in the year. Prior to his arrival he had unsuccessfully endeavoured to get the organ from the Panopticon in London for the Ulster Hall.

Chipp's appointment was announced in London and the notice

repeated in the *Belfast News-Letter.*[36] This referred to a presentation to him from his last London post, Trinity Church, Paddington, of a testimonial and a silver tea and coffee service. Belfast seemed to be honoured by the appointment, and the *Musical World* notice regretted his leaving London in the following terms:

> *The fact of Dr. Chipp's abandoning London as the sphere of his professional exertions, in favour of a country town, even though that country town is Belfast itself, the most musical in musical Ireland, must therefore be seriously regretted. We have not so many earnest labourers among us that we can afford to lose one of the most earnest and gifted of them all.*[37]

In August 1862 the *News-Letter* announced that Chipp would arrive in October and 'superintend the erection of the organ,'[38] but the same paper regretted later that month that the date of the Festival had yet to be announced, even though the organ was almost ready

The Mulholland Grand Organ, Ulster Hall, Belfast, c. 1863 (courtesy of the National Library of Ireland)

to be erected.[39] The Belfast Musical Festival was held over two days, 17 and 18 December 1862, under the patronage of the Lord Lieutenant, the Earl of Carlisle. The organ was inaugurated on the Wednesday evening with a concert including an 'Organ Inauguration Ode' composed by Chipp, with words supplied by the Reverend William McIlwaine of St. George's Church (Annex 5). Orchestral players from London included Chipp's brother Horatio, cello, and his father Thomas, drums. Members of the Bradford Chorus strengthened local singing forces.

In the usual adulatory fashion the concert was reviewed the following day in the *Belfast News-Letter*[40] and every detail recorded, even the fact that after the Viceregal party had entered (late) the first verse of the National Anthem was played, after which, following a suitable modulation, the second verse was sung by the altos before the third verse resumed in the original key. Chipp then left the rostrum to preside at the organ for the 'Inauguration Ode'. The reviewer thought that Chipp's strength as a composer lay in his writing for massed choral forces rather than in writing for the solo voice in the recitative and aria. The organ itself had a prominent part in the work. Beethoven's *Fidelio* overture followed, with other overtures and sundry vocal items. Wilbye Cooper was again a soloist. Chipp's own *God Preserve the Emperor* variations, with Bach's Fugue in G minor as an encore, and Handel's 'Let their celestial concerts' concluded the event. The review recorded the following comments on Chipp's celebrated variations:

> *The first of these performances was God preserve the Emperor, with variations by Dr. Chipp himself. The astonishing acquirements of the performer as a pedallist were in this solo exhibited to perfection. Rapid passages and intricate variations were played by the two feet, which crossed over each other, and flew from side to side and from note to note with an agility that often baffled the keenest eyes, and might have been envied by the most accomplished reel-dancer that was ever attached to a Scottish clan.*

> *Nor were his hands idle. The grasp of the instrument, if we may so say, which Dr. Chipp took, asserted itself from the first. He could call any one of the three thousand pipes to his assistance at will, and the noble instrument, a giant amongst its brethren, was obedient to every touch of the master. From soft, and almost vocal combinations it changed, under his hand, to a wild tempest of tumultuous sounds, all answering their purpose, indeed, and all grandly characteristic; and then, again, it died away in sweet and appealing harmonies, until its closing notes were lost amid a burst of genuine applause.*[41]

18 December saw another concert of mixed items: overtures: a cello solo by Horatio Chipp, vocal items and two organ solos, Mendelssohn's second sonata and Chipp's variations on 'The Harmonious Blacksmith', followed by part-songs from the Bradford Chorus singers. The concert had begun at 1 pm and only ended at 4 pm. The indefatigable conductor and musicians concluded the festival that evening with a performance of Haydn's *Creation*, and large crowds had gathered around the entrances long before the hall opened. The oratorio concluded at eleven o'clock and Chipp played on the organ between the second and third parts.[42] Although the organ had now been inaugurated, it was not finally completed until January 1863, when William Hill came to give the final touches.[43]

The Saturdays of 20 and 27 December saw concerts by Chipp for the benefit of the working classes, but despite the price for admission to the main body of the hall being lowered from 6d to 3d for the second one, the working classes did not fulfil their part in the enterprise by turning up in great numbers. In all Chipp gave fifty-seven solo recitals in his first season as Organist of the Ulster Hall, for which he received £300.[44] Arrangements of orchestral and choral music provided the bulk of the fare during the first season, but there were many Bach preludes and fugues and all six of the Mendelssohn sonatas. In 1864 the concerts resumed, presumably after a pause, and the night was changed to Monday, again to try to attract the working classes. On one of these occasions he played Meyerbeer arrangements and was 'warmly applauded.'[45] The idea of fostering musical education in Belfast was obviously something that Chipp wanted to pursue, part of a general trend at the time along with the introduction of town hall organs. However, the project to conduct a class for 'the instruction of the people in music' at a moderate charge was not successful.[46] He then announced a class 'for the performance of chamber music and choruses' in conjunction with Mr. H.J. Loveday. These 'Quartette [sic] Subscription Concerts' were more successful. Mendelssohn quartets, songs and other chamber music were featured in the third one, held on 12 February 1864. The concert also included Chipp's song 'My sailor boy at sea', which appeared to be widely known at that time from press advertisements. Of the composer and organiser of the concert it was noted, 'Of Dr. Chipp it is needless to speak, for his praise is in every mouth. He was the life and moving power of these concerts.'[47] Chipp's farewell concert in Belfast was on 26 January 1866, which saw a performance of Mendelssohn's *Elijah* by the Belfast Vocal Union, which Chipp had founded.[47]

As early as August 1865 the *Dundee Courier* reported that 'Dr. E. Chipp of Belfast ... is a candidate for the Chair of Music, Edinburgh.'[48] His name does not appear, however, in the list of twenty-one candidates reported in *The Choir*.[49] A long article appeared in the *Belfast News-Letter* in January 1866 lamenting the announcement of his departure from Belfast.[50] One extract will suffice:

> *With an unblemished reputation, and a zeal in the pursuit to which he had attached himself from his earliest years, Dr. E.T. Chipp was welcomed by all the lovers of music to Belfast, as a real boon of the cultivation of 'the divine art.*

It notes 'the offer from a Scottish provincial town to act as their organist with duties light and well paid,' and it would seem the remuneration offered was more advantageous than had apparently been requested of his directors in Belfast. The article concluded with a plea to the members of the Vocal Union to make an effort to retain their founder. The stage was set for Chipp's move to Scotland.

Before he left Belfast, however, it was assured that Chipp's work and influence at St. George's Church should not be forgotten. On 11 October 1863, only a year after his arrival, a new organ by J.W. Walker was opened there. Prior to Chipp's arrival the music at the church had not been of the best and the organ was in a poor state, in addition to which the church was to undergo a programme of repairs. Whilst the church restoration was being carried out, services were held in the Ulster Hall with Chipp at the organ. At the reopening service, the redoubtable organist had assembled a choir of sixty voices, who sang an anthem by Mendelssohn, and some of Chipp's own chants and settings were used. The occasion was seen in the review as inaugurating 'a new era of church music in Belfast.'[51] The new organ (two manuals and pedals) had twenty-seven stops, was designed by Chipp, and was described in the above review as 'for church purposes, perfection.'

7
A Scottish Interlude

The offer from a Scottish provincial town referred to earlier was from Lord Kinnaird, after whom the Kinnaird Hall in Dundee was named. In January 1866 he wrote to the *Dundee Advertiser* to clarify his announcement to the Hall Association about the appointment of an organist.[52] After applications had been received, the

Forster & Andrews organ, Kinnaird Hall, Dundee, 1865 (Wilson Collection, Local History Centre, Dundee Central Library)

Directors heard that there was a possibility of Chipp leaving Belfast, and one of them asked him to confirm this. As a result Chipp was appointed. Lord Kinnaird did not wish the impression to be gained that Chipp had actually applied for the post. The organ installed in 1865 was a four-manual instrument by Forster & Andrews with forty-nine stops, and the cost was £1,300. It was understood at the time that the specification was drawn up by the German organ builder Edmund Schulze. The date of the opening of the organ is not known, nor is the date at which Chipp actually took up his appointment; it is known, however, that it was opened by N.J. Lemmens, the Belgian organist, and not by Chipp. Lemmens declared, 'he had never played upon a better instrument in the United Kingdom'.[53]

Today the Hall and organ are gone, but Edmund Chipp's memory lingers on in press reports. The second and third of a subscription series of concerts took place on 19 and 20 March 1866. The reporter of the first concert thought Chipp's own 'Pastorale' (one of the *24 Sketches*) the 'sweetest and most tasteful piece of the evening.'[54] At the third concert he played his own variations on 'The Harmonious Blacksmith', as well as arrangements from operas.[55]

Although Chipp returned to England at the end of 1866, his farewell concert in Dundee was held on 19th March, 1867. The press report regretted that the Hall was not completely packed for the occasion:

> *Looking to the fact of its being the farewell appearance of the town's organist, a gentleman so distinguished in his profession that the town has very great reason to be proud of such a connection ... Dr. Chipp's first appearance was the signal for a round of hearty cheering.*[56]

A pupil of Chipp's, Isabella Andrews, sang a song by Mendelssohn and also the organist's own song 'My sailor boy at sea.' Although this song is not among the known surviving manuscript music, it is possible that it reappears later as 'The Seaman's Song' with words by his son Herbert, dated July 1874.

Biographical sources state that Chipp was organist of St. Paul's Church, Edinburgh, from May to November 1866, and his obituary confirms his residence in Edinburgh, but no details of this short appointment have been found.[57]

8
THE ELY YEARS

Edmund Chipp was elected and sworn in as Organist and *Magister Choristarum* of Ely Cathedral on 14 June 1867.[58] A note in a manuscript copy of 'O clap your hands,' a setting of Psalm 47 for double choir, written in Edinburgh in 1866, says 'sung for the first time in Ely Cathedral, February 5, 1867.' It would seem therefore that Chipp was carrying out his duties before he was formally elected, and this may be accounted for by the fact that the Chapter met infrequently. Names of applicants had been received in November 1866, the previous Organist Robert Janes having died in the autumn, and the choice left to the Dean and Chapter. The Chapter records for 28 October 1868 reveal:

> *Dr. Chipp having attended and having represented to the Chapter that the house erected for him was in several respects unsuited to his requirements agreed that the sum of £20 per annum be allowed to Dr. Chipp for house rent and that Dr. Chipp return the keys of the new house to the Dean.*[59]

The alternative house which Chipp preferred was to be his home for the rest of his life, and the inscription 'Palace Green, Ely' duly appeared at the end of compositions thereafter. The 1871 Census showed that at that time, apart from himself, his wife, son Herbert and daughter Emily, there were four other members of his household. The intended but unused new house had been built next to the Porter's Lodge.

On Chipp's arrival, Canon W.E. Dickson (Precentor), who had been invited to assume the office of *Magister Choristarum* in 1858, surrendered these duties, although he deputised in Chipp's absence. Both born in the same year, Dickson and Chipp must have had a great deal to share of mutual interest, given Dickson's keen interest in church music and organs. The Choir School at Ely had been put on a permanent and satisfactory footing by Dean Goodwin through the appointment of a certificated master who had had charge of the Choir School at Cambridge maintained jointly by Trinity and St. John's Colleges.[60] A Choristers' School had been created in 1859 on land near the Sacrists' Gate. Dean Goodwin himself recounted Chipp playing in the Cathedral at night:

> *On a summer's evening, full moon by choice, he would invite us to listen to a little music in the Cathedral. The effect was thrilling ... Beethoven's so-called Moonlight Sonata, Schubert's Ave Maria and some of Bach's Fugues, rise to my memory with special delight.*[61]

Other pieces played at such times, i.e. after 9 pm, recorded by Chipp himself in annotations on manuscript copies include 'Lift thine eyes' from Mendelssohn's *Elijah* for violin and violas, and his own *God Preserve the Emperor* variations arranged for violin and viola, both on the same occasion, 20 January 1877.

Services were expanded at that time, and music of a high class (according to Precentor Dickson) added, such as Haydn's *Seven Last Words*, and *Calvary* and *Last Judgement* by Spohr, perhaps in themselves a commentary on what had gone before:

> *The accompaniments were skilfully played by E.T. Chipp who succeeded in overcoming the serious difficulty created by the distance intervening between the organ in the Quire and singers in the Octagon.*[62]

Dickson's reference to the distance between the organ in the Quire and singers in the Octagon relates to the fact that in 1851 William

Hill had placed an organ in the north choir triforium with a case incorporating parts of the organ overhanging the choir, although the keyboards were placed further back under the triforium vaulting. This had replaced the organ on the stone screen in the presbytery dating from 1770.[63] To this day, the organ in the Quire accompanies both services held in the Quire and those held in the main body of the Cathedral with the singers under the Octagon. The organ envisaged in 1851 was finally completed and enlarged by Hill in 1867, and opened on 24 June 1867, the Feast of St. John the Baptist. A feature of the 'new' organ was the 32ft Pedal Bourdon, a gift from the people of Ely. Choristers from Norwich, Cambridge and Peterborough joined the Cathedral Choir. Chipp gave a recital after the service, including his usual fare of Mendelssohn, Bach, arrangements from Beethoven, Mozart, Pleyel, Rossini and Handel, with 'Ave Maria', one of the *24 Sketches*. One press report stated:

> *Of Dr. Chipp's great ability as an organist there is no question, however tastes may differ as to his style, and he did the fullest justice to the above selection.*[64]

It would seem that the unusual mechanical layout at that time involved a great deal of physical effort from the player, which Chipp himself complained of.[65]

In 1869 Dickson recorded that the second weekly choir rehearsal was given up after long and painful disputation at the instance of Mr. Jane's successor.[66] Chipp was allowed an assistant from 1880 onwards, who received £20 a year. During his time as Organist the Choristers were likely to have been up to twenty in number, thanks to Precentor Dickson's efforts, with up to eight Lay Clerks.

A quite remarkable event during Chipp's tenure at Ely must have been the five days of celebrations of the Bissexcentenary Festival of St. Etheldreda (founder of the Abbey at Ely) held in the Cathedral from Friday 17 October to Tuesday 21 October 1873, which

Ely Cathedral organ, *Musical Times*, 1 March 1902 (courtesy of Cambridge University Library)

included the Fourteenth Annual Festival of the Ely Diocesan Church Music Society. *The Musical Times* stated:

> *Whilst speaking of the anniversary services it may be remarked that an admirable illustration of the state of Cathedral Music at the present day was furnished, Sir John Goss, Dr. Wesley, Dr. Stainer, Mr. E.J. Hopkins, Mr. H. Smart, Mr. Barnby, Dr. Garrett, Mr. J. Baptiste Calkin, Dr. Chipp (Organist to the Cathedral) and Mr. G.F. Jackman, formerly a chorister being fairly represented by their works.*[67]

The orders of service over the five days are appended at Annex 4 in order to illustrate what a marathon the whole event must have been. Chipp's anthem in honour of St. Etheldreda composed by request for the Festival, 'The Lord hath been mindful of us', based on verses from Psalm 115, was sung on the Friday morning at the service of Matins. His Gloria setting was sung at the Holy Communion service on the same morning. A service setting and his anthem 'The earth shall be full of the knowledge of the Lord' were sung on the Sunday morning. Chipp himself gave an organ recital at 9.30 pm on the Saturday, from which it may be seen that almost every item was a transcription (see Annex 4).

Another mammoth occasion, although this time only lasting one day, but with a morning and afternoon service, was the Triennial Choral Festival of the Ely Diocesan Church Music Society in June 1867. Eleven hundred voices from twenty-five choirs took part, and processed from the west end to the Octagon and transepts singing, 'Advance! Advance!' composed for the occasion by Dr. Chipp, who presided at the organ. The band of the Cambridge Militia contributed their assistance to the accompaniment from the triforium. Chipp gave a recital after the second service.[68]

A more domestic Ely composition was a song 'A silver festival greeting' occasioned by the Silver Wedding of the Dean of Ely and Mrs. Merivale on 2 July 1875, which survives in manuscript form.

During Chipp's tenure at Ely, the nearby Parish Church of St. Mary acquired in 1879-80 the organ built in 1846 for the London Church of Holy Trinity, Paddington, where Chipp had been Organist from 1856 to 1862. This was doubtless due to his influence. A survival from the English classical tradition of organ building, the organ is now in its third home at All Saints' Church, Haslingfield, Cambridgeshire, where some of his music has been recorded.[69]

One of Chipp's pupils at Ely was the sixteen-year-old W.G. Price, who four years later became Organist of St. George's Church, Belfast, a post that Chipp had previously occupied. Dr. Price eventually emigrated to Melbourne, Australia, where he became City Organist and gave the opening recital on the 1929 organ in Melbourne Town Hall on 3 July of that year.[70] Another articled pupil at Ely from 1880 to 83 was Alfred George Macey, later organist of St. Barnabas Church, Dartmouth.[71]

Amongst Edmund Chipp's activities during this phase of his life was acting as examiner for Bachelor of Music degrees for Cambridge University (along with G.A. Macfarren and C.V. Stanford).[72] He also acted as an examiner for Trinity College London.[73] A concert by Chipp at nearby Littleport in Cambridgeshire was noted in 1883.[74]

It is clear from the various reviews of his concerts that Chipp was highly regarded in his day as an organist, and this is confirmed in his obituary: 'Dr. Chipp's eminent abilities placed him in the first rank of organists.'[75] The *Musical World* seems to have been particularly well disposed towards him in its reviews and in its defence of him at the time of his involvement with Her Majesty's Private Band, but in any case he was obviously well thought of as a musician. His own organ compositions take their place in the tradition following on from the visits to England and subsequent influence of Felix Mendelssohn, and have an integrity of their own which deserves wider recognition today. He was also interested in organs themselves, having been involved or associated with the installation of a number of instruments during the course of his life. There was also clearly a talent for organisation evident in his association with large-scale musical events such as those in Belfast, and the St. Etheldreda celebrations in Ely, and evidence of considerable energy in encouraging and creating music in the places where he worked. His was certainly a 'life that led melodious days,' encompassing as it did the transition during the nineteenth century from the role of an all-round musician who happened to play the organ, more prevalent in the eighteenth century, to that of the specialist cathedral and church organist which we know today.

Notes

Abbreviations

EDC Ely Dean and Chapter Archives, Cambridge University Library

JBIOS *Journal of the British Institute of Organ Studies*

1. National Archives, 1841 Census.
2. *Musical Times*, 1 February 1887, p. 100, from which all biographical information is taken; the Mus.D. award appeared in the *Norfolk Chronicle*, 30 June 1860; Chipp's personal estate amounted to £732, later amended to £947.
3. Parish Registers, St. John's Church, Hampstead.
4. *Musical Times*, 1 February 1887.
5. EDC 14/45.
6. Thistlethwaite, N., 'Reforming organists: the Cooper family of St. Sepulchre's, Holborn,' *JBIOS*, 34, 2010, pp. 82–115, p. 101.
7. *Musical Times*, 1900, vol. 41, p. 315.
8. *Musical World*, 1860, vol. 38, p. 465.
9. *Musical World*, 23 December 1865, vol. 43, p. 805.
10. Scholes, P., *The Mirror of Music*, London, Novello & Co., 1947.
11. *Musical Times*, 1 December 1901, pp. 794-97.

12. *Musical World*, 15 September 1849, 577–78.
13. *The London Pianoforte School 1766–1860*, N. Temperley, ed., New York and London, Garland, 1985.
14. *Musical World*, 5 February 1859, pp. 82–86.
15. McCann Collection, Royal Academy of Music, 2005.1445.
16. *Musical World*, 5 February 1859, p. 323.
17. *Musical Times*, 1 September 1870, p. 606.
18. EDC 14/26.
19. Glover, W., *Memoirs of a Cambridge Chorister*, vol. 2, p. 240.
20. *Belfast News-Letter*, 22 December 1862.
21. Report of the Executive Committee, Exhibition of Art Treasures of the United Kingdom, held at Manchester, 1857, originally published 1859.
22. *Musical World*, 24 October 1857, p. 688.
23. *Musical Times*, 15 December 1854, p. 247.
24. *Musical World*, 17 November 1859.
25. *Leicester Mercury*, 20 October 1860.
26. Elvin, L., *Forster and Andrews, their Barrel, Chamber and Small Church Organs*, 1976.
27. *Belfast News-Letter*, 5 November 1862.
28. *Hertford Mercury and Reformer*, 10 October 1857.
29. *Belfast News-Letter*, 5 November 1862; for further information about the organ see Elvin, L. in *The Organ*, July 1962, p. 21.
30. *Hertfordshire Guardian*, 1 November 1862.
31. *Musical World*, March–June 1855.

32. *Musical World*, 21 July 1855.
33. *Musical World*, 2 February 1856.
34. *The Morning Post*, 26 February 1856.
35. *Belfast News-Letter*, 18 December 1862.
36. *Belfast News-Letter*, 5 November 1862.
37. *Musical World*, 25 October 1862.
38. *Belfast News-Letter*, 2 August 1862.
39. *Belfast News-Letter*, 16 August 1862.
40. *Belfast News-Letter*, 18 December 1862; additional details appeared in *Musical World*, 3 January 1863, pp. 5-6.
41. *Belfast News-Letter*, 18 December 1862.
42. *Belfast News-Letter*, 19 December 1862.
43. *Belfast News-Letter*, 10 January 1863.
44. Johnston, R., unpublished Ph.D. dissertation, *The Musical Life of Belfast to 1874*, 1999.
45. *Musical World*, 10 September 1864.
46. *Belfast News-Letter*, 13 February 1864.
47. *Musical Times*, 1 March 1866.
48. *Dundee Courier*, 21 August 1865.
49. *The Choir*, 1 November 1865.
50. *Belfast News-Letter*, 5 January 1866.
51. *Musical World*, 24 October 1863
52. *Dundee Advertiser*, 5 January 1866
53. Elvin, L., *Forster and Andrews, Organ Builders 1843-1956*, 1968

54. *Dundee Advertiser*, 20 March 1866
55. *Dundee Advertiser*, 24 March 1866
56. *Dundee Courier*, 20 March 1867
57. *Dictionary of National Biography*, 1885-1900, vol. 10, and *Musical Times*, 1 February 1887.
58. EDC 2/2/A/7.
59. *Ibid.*
60. Dean Goodwin, *Ely Gossip* (Ely Cathedral Archives).
61. *Ibid.*
62. Dickson, W.E., *50 Years of Church Music*, Ely, 1894
63. For further information on organs in Ely Cathedral up to 1851 see Hopkins, J., *JBIOS*, 21, pp. 4-19, 1997.
64. *Bury and Norwich Post*, 2 July 1867.
65. Thistlethwaite, N.J. *The Organs and Organists of Ely Cathedral* (no date).
66. Dickson, *op. cit.*
67. *Musical Times*, 1 November 1873, p. 280.
68. *Bury and Norwich Post*, 20 June 1867.
69. www.npor.org.uk/C00877 (BIOS Historic Organ Sound Archive).
70. Information derived from *The Advertiser*, Adelaide (online).
71. Royal Society of Musicians membership register.
72. *The Morning Post*, 5 December 1881.
73. *Buckinghamshire Herald*, 7 August 1880.
74. *Musical Opinion*, 1 February 1883.
75. *Musical Times*, 1 February 1887.

Annex 1

E.T. Chipp: 24 Sketches for the Organ, Op. 11, 1855

1. Andante religioso in D
2. In memoriam M.F.G.C. in B minor
3. Con moto in G
4. Adagio ma non troppo in E♭
5. Con moto molto tranquillo in G minor
6. Andante tranquillo in B♭
7. Andante e molto sostenuto in E♭ minor
8. Con moto ma non troppo presto in E♭
9. Con moto molto tranquillo in B minor
10. Canzonet in G
11. Lento in E
12. Pastorale in A
13. In memoriam F.M.B. in C♯ minor
14. Larghetto in E
15. Moderato e tranquillo in A
16. Andante con moto in F♯ minor
17. Moderato e sostenuto in D
18. Andante non troppo in G
19. In memoriam M.F.G.C. in F minor, molto adagio e lento
20. Grazioso in F
21. Andante maestoso in B♭ minor
22. Moderato e legato in B♭
23. Andante e sostenuto in A minor (set of variations)
24. Ave Maria in A

Annex 2

E.T. Chipp: Published original organ works

Op. 1	Variations on 'The Harmonious Blacksmith', 1848, Novello, Inscribed to E.J. Hopkins of the Temple Church
Op. 2	Variations on 'God Preserve the Emperor,' 1849, D'Almaine For the Birmingham Festival
Op. 3	Introduction and Melody Varied for the Organ, Ewer Inscribed to G.J. Elvey
Op. 7	Three Studies, 1854, Ewer
Op. 8	Three Sketches, 1853, Graue & Co.
Op. 11	24 Sketches, Subscribers' Edition, 1855, Ewer (nos. 1-12 ed. Mansfield, 1936)

Compositions for the Organ, Subscribers' Edition, 1888, ed. Garrett & Higgs

Compositions for the Organ, Bk. 2, *Miscellaneous Solos*, 1936, ed. Mansfield

Four Organ Pieces

1. O Sanctissima with two variations and finale
2. Andante con moto
3. Intermezzo
4. Fugue in A minor

Adagio in E (in *The Village Organist*), 1875

Note: Some pieces appeared in later anthologies, and digitised versions are now appearing in print (as of July 2013).

Annex 3

Specification of the Kirtland & Jardine organ built for the Art Treasures exhibition, Manchester, 1857

APPENDIX No. XVIII.

GRAND ORGAN.

Description of the Grand Organ erected and placed at the service of the Executive Committee by Messrs. Kirtland and Jardine, *of Dickinson St, Manchester.—Organist,* Mr. Henry Walker.

It consisted of three rows of keys, and a pedal clavier, upon which the stops were thus disposed:—

GREAT ORGAN, COMPASS CC TO G IN ALTISSIMO, 56 NOTES.

No.	Stop	Pitch	No.	Stop	Pitch
1	Double diapason...	16 feet.	9	Clear flute	4 feet.
2	Full open diapason...	8 "	10	Twelfth...	2⅔ "
3	Violin open diapason.... ...	8 "	11	Fifteenth	2 "
4	Höhl-flöte	8 "	12	Mixture, 5 ranks	
5	Stopped diapason	8 "	13	Double trumpet	16 "
6	Quint	5⅓ "	14	Posaune	8 "
7	Principal	4 "	15	Clarion	4 "
8	Gamba	4 "			

CHOIR ORGAN, COMPASS CC TO G IN ALTISSIMO, 56 NOTES.

No.	Stop	Pitch	No.	Stop	Pitch
16	Lieblich gedacht	8 feet.	20	Bassoon	8 feet.
17	Dulciana	8 "	21	Clarinet	8 "
18	Voix celeste	8 "	22	Voix humaine	8 "
19	Röhr flöte	4 "			

SWELL ORGAN, COMPASS CC TO G IN ALTISSIMO, 56 NOTES.

No.	Stop	Pitch	No.	Stop	Pitch
23	Bourdon	16 feet.	30	Fifteenth	2 feet.
24	Open diapason	8 "	31	Clear Mixture, 5 ranks	
25	Gedacht	8 "	32	Euphone (free reed)	16 "
26	Keraulophon	8 "	33	Cornopean	8 "
27	Principal	4 "	34	Oboe	8 "
28	Höhl flöte	4 "	35	Clarion	4 "
29	Twelfth	2⅔ "			

PEDAL ORGAN, COMPASS CCC TO E, 29 NOTES.

No.	Stop	Pitch	No.	Stop	Pitch
36	Sub-bass	32 feet.	41	Violoncello	8 feet.
37	Open diapason	16 "	42	Twelfth	5⅓ "
38	Bourdon	16 "	53	Fifteenth	4 "
39	Grosse quint	10⅔ "	44	Posaune (free reed)	16 "
40	Principal	8 "	45	Trumpet...	8 „

COUPLERS AND ACCESSORY STOPS.

No.	Stop	No.	Stop
46	Swell to great organ, sub octave.	51	Great organ to pedal.
47	" " " unison.	52	Choir " "
48	" " " octave.	53	Tremulant to choir organ.
49	Choir to great organ.	54	" " "
50	Swell to organ and pedal.		

Annex 4

Orders of Service, Bissexcentenary Festival of St. Etheldreda, Ely Cathedral 1873

THE

Bissexcentenary Festival of St. Etheldreda,

AT ELY.

Friday, October 17th,

St. Etheldreda.

9 0, a.m. Litany.

11 0, a.m. Matins.

Special Lessons, 1 Sam. ii. 10—18. Acts ii. 37—47.

Te Deum, Jubilate, } *Garrett in D.*

Anthem—"The Lord hath been mindful of us."—*Chipp.*

Hymns—Process. and Recess.—"To the Name of our salvation."

Address to the Clergy by the Right Rev. the Lord Bishop of the Diocese.*

12 30, p.m. Holy Communion.

Introit, *Hymn iii.* From Festival Book.

Kyrie, Credo, } *Garrett in D.*

Gloria, *Chipp in D.*

1 30, p.m. Luncheon at the Bishop's Palace for the Clergy of the Isle of Ely.

3 30, p.m. Even-song.

Special Lessons, 2 Sam. vii. 18—29. Rev. xxii.

Magnificat, Nunc Dimittis, } *Garrett in D.*

Anthems, { "My heart is inditing." Hallelujah Chorus. } *Handel.*

Address by the Very Rev. the Dean.†

---

* See p. 5. † See p. 7.

In the evening Entertainments were given to the College Officials, Tenants, and College Tradesmen at the Lamb Hotel: to the National School Managers and Teachers at the Bell Hotel: to the Choristers at their School: to the Bedesmen, College Servants, Parents of National School Children and others, at the Corn Exchange.

Address by Archdeacon Emery.*

Address by the Bishop.†

Saturday, October 18th,

St. Luke.

10 0, a.m. Matins.

Te Deum, Jubilate, } *Barnby in E.*

Introit, *Hymn 142 (3).*

Kyrie, Credo, } *Barnby in E.*

Anthem—"The righteous live."—*Stainer.*

The Rev. Canon Selwyn delivered an address‡ to the National School Children who attended service in a body.

4 0, p.m. Even-song.

Magnificat, Nunc Dimittis, } *Barnby in E.*

Anthem—"Hear my prayer."—*Mendelssohn.*

9 30, p.m. Recital in the Cathedral by Dr. Chipp, the Organist.

The following pieces were played on the organ:

Overture.—Occasional Oratorio .... *Handel.*
Adagio—Scotch Symphonie .... *Mendelssohn.*
Pastorale .... *Corelli.*
Fugue in D major .... *Bach.*
Larghetto—Clarinet Quintet .... *Mozart.*
Triumphal March .... *Beethoven.*
Andante Movement .... *Haydn.*
Prayer from Mosé in Egitto .... *Rossini.*
Dead March in Saul .... *Handel.*

* See p. 18. † See p. 20. ‡ See p. 26.

Sunday, October 19th.

9 0, a.m. Litany.

11 0, a.m. Matins.

Te Deum, Jubilate, } *Chipp in D.*

Anthem—"The earth shall be full of the knowledge of the Lord."—*Chipp.*

Sermon by the Right Rev. the Lord Bishop of the Diocese*

Processional Hymn—"Sweet place." *From Festival Book.*

Recessional Hymn—"Onward, Christian Soldiers." *From Festival Book.*

1 0, p.m. Holy Communion.

Introit, *Hymn 139.*

Kyrie, Credo, } *Jackman in E flat.*

Gloria,

2 45, p.m. Litany in Trinity Church.

Sermon by Rev. Canon Kingsley.†

4 0, p.m. Even-song.

Magnificat. Nunc Dimittis, } *Attwood in C.*

Anthem—"O come, let us sing."—*Handel.*

6 30, p.m. Service in the Nave, with voluntary choir.

Sermon by the Right Rev. the Lord Bishop of Peterborough.‡

Monday, October 20th.

10 0, a.m. Matins.

Te Deum, Jubilate, } *Hopkins in A.*

Anthem—"Stand up and bless the Lord."—*Goss.*

12 0, m. Lecture on the Cathedral by Sir Gilbert Scott, A.R.A. Architect,§ delivered by his son, Mr. G. Scott, M.A.

Tour of the Cathedral, directed by Mr. Edmund Sharpe, M.A.‖

1 30, p.m. Addresses presented to the Bishop by the Chapter, and Archdeaconries of the Diocese.¶

---

* See p. 29. † See p. 39. ‡ See p. 40. § See p. 47. ‖ See p. 70. ¶ See p. 72.

2 30, p.m. Collation for invited guests in the Corn Exchange.*

5 0, p.m. Even-song.

Magnificat, Nunc Dimittis, } *Hopkins in F.*

Anthem—"Ascribe unto the Lord."—*S. S. Wesley.*

8 0, p.m. Reception at the Bishop's Palace.

Tuesday, October 21st.

11 0, a.m. Matins. Festival music.

Te Deum, *Smart in F.*

Anthems { "Sing praises unto the Lord."—*Gounod.* "Judge me, O God."—*Mendelssohn.*

Meeting of Diocesan Choirs in the Nave.

Address by the Right Rev. the Lord Bishop of the Diocese.†

Processional Hymn—"Sweet place."

Recessional Hymn—"Onward, Christian Soldiers."

Accompanied by the Band of the Cambridgeshire Militia, stationed in the north Triforium.

2 30, p.m. Even-song.

Meeting of Diocesan Parish Choirs in the Nave.

Magnificat, Nunc Dimittis, } *S. S. Wesley in F.*

Anthems and Hymns as in the morning.

Sermon by the Right Rev. the Lord Bishop of Bath and Wells.‡

4 30, p.m. Tea for Choirs in the Corn Exchange.

Appendix.—Historical Summary, a.d. 673-1873.§

* See p. 71. † See p. 88. ‡ See p. 89. § See p. 94.

Annex 5

Organ Inauguration Ode

CHORUS
Where the limpid river gliding
Bears its tribute to the main,
Where the dews of morn abiding
Clothe with corn the smiling plain:
Upward rise adoring voices,
Praising God, all-wise, all-good,
Universal earth rejoices,
Surging sea, and waving wood.
Praise His name in sounding chorus,
Swell the organ's tuneful voice;
Praise Him for His goodness o'er us,
For His mercies past rejoice.
Praise Him, all ye mighty nations,
From all oceans, through all lands;
Praise Him with our minds' creations,
With the labour of your hands!

RECITATIVE
Hardy sons of toil,
Sage of soaring reason,
Brothers, cease to moil,
Rest ye here a season,
High and low unite,
Hearts and voices blended,
Join our festal rite,
Feud and action ended,
Banish care and pain,
Smooth the brow of sadness;
Raise the choral strain,
Roll the tide of gladness.

ARIA
Thus crown we him whose generous care
Is spent the sons of toil to raise,
Nor war's proud trophies may compare
With this our meed of peaceful praise,
Let distant ages learn his name
Whose wealth to bless his kind is given;
And, as we raise the loud acclaim,
Around him shed the smile of Heaven!

CHORUS
Praise the God that dwelleth
In the realms of light;
Praise His name who telleth
All the stars of night
Roll your notes of thunder,
Cloud and storm above;
Praise the God of wonder,
Laud the God of love.
Sons of men, adore Him,
Sound His praises high;
Lowly bend before Him,
Earth, and sea, and sky!

Words by Rev. W. McIlwaine (from *Belfast News-Letter*, 18 December 1862)
Music by Dr. E.T. Chipp

Notes

Notes